Breaking Through:

CHANGING THE NARRATIVE

Ken L. Ross

Ken L. Ross
Klross1030@gmail.com

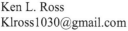 @breakingthrough  @kross1030 @Ken Ross MS

Book Layout ©2019 Ken's Koncept's

Ordering Information:
Quantity sales. Special discounts are available on quantity purchases by corporations, associations, and others. For details, contact the author at klross1030@gmail.com.

Breaking Through: Changing the Narrative/ Ken L. Ross. −1st ed.
ISBN 13: 978-0-578-51411-6

Contents

I dedicate this book to my mother

Dorothy Ross

Who have always inspired me to be great

With a powerful desire, with a strong determination, and with a commitment to yourself, you can find ways to achieve your goals, and overcome challenges.

—Catherine Pulsifer

Introduction

This book is written to present functionally real-life situation where relevant and informative information is shared and learned that will give the reader an opportunity to grow and develop techniques and strategies to exercise when confronted with complex life situations. The information is designed to consolidate building blocks of learning information and techniques that would strengthen their growth by providing them a step by step process that can easily be understood and practice.

The aim of this book is to be a working manual script, reinforcing the information presented by the writer in his first book *"Breaking Throught: Winning*

Against the Odds". It is encouraged that you also read this book as well.

This book is not designed to provide a detailed explanation of all aspects of the challenges you will face navigating through some of the obstacles towards becoming a successful, respectful citizen contributing to the development of society and humanity, nor does it have all the answers for our returning citizens who will have a hard time struggling to reintegrate back into society.

However, this book is designed upon these 8 characteristics:

Cultural Consciousness   Self-Awareness

Manhood   Relationship Building

Human Development   Spirituality

Discipline   Goal Setting

Book Objectives

By the end of this book, you will be able to:

• Understand the correlation and rational behind community violence

• Understand methods of conflict resolution

• Understand the methology of the criminal justice system

• Use a variety of tools to navigate the challenges of life

• Understand how your socio-physical environment effects your development

• Understanding your role as a father/man

• Develop effective styles of communication

• Set goals and plan ahead

• Insight on Self-awareness

• Developed self-discipline

• Develop positive relationships

And, much, much more. This book is written holistically to deal with the overall person and the many challenges that you may face during your struggle to be successful in all your endeavors.

KEN L. ROSS

BREAKING THROUGH
CHANGING THE NARRATIVE

KEN L. ROSS
Breaking Through: Changing the Narrative
Ken's Koncepts ™
klross1030@gmail.com
P.O. Box 19601
Chicago, Illinois 60619
Phone 630-708-6372

Positive results for students will come from changes in the knowledge, skills, and behavior they inherit. We must provide the opportunity, support, incentive, and expectations for our young people to live as children and make wise decisions as they grow into adult.

[1]

INTRODUCTION TO BREAKING THROUGH:
Changing the Narrative

This book was written to help young men around the country who face all kinds of adversities growing up in our society that is filtrated with drugs, guns and violence. As I mentioned in my previous book *"Breaking Through: Winning Against the Odds"* successful navigation through these challenges is based upon a mindset. It is my hope in this book *"Changing the Narrative",* is that I share information to help them develop a concrete structured life plan consistent with positive goal setting that will guide them and give them insight on some life changing techniques that will inspire and motivate them to detour away from the life of the streets and sub-culture of society that perpetuate violence and drug usage. By the end of this book it is my hope that they will reconsidered the identity that they have adopted or inherited; developed a sense of culture and establishes core values; be able to set goals and prioritizes education as important and strive to reach their fullest potential, and those who are reading for clearer direction and clarity on some of the social issue effecting this population and seeking guidance will have a clearer understanding on what to do as parents, teachers, guidance counselors or group facilitators.

This book is written with ten chapters, the first five chapters of this book is written from a socio-psychological perspective and is structured to address our thinking process. So, before we get off into the core of the book, I feel that we must first talk about and address some of the dynamics that is shaping and affecting the mentality of violence in our society and the correlation of social conditions to causes and effects.

The second part of the book addresses the changing process. This part of the book is key for the effective implementation of life changing outcomes.

Why This Book Was Written:

Breaking Through: Changing the Narrative is a book of self-intervention, and individual growth and development. This book includes a psycho-educational 'like' format along with a style of therapeutic analysis. This book was designed for correctional facilities, schools and community-based programs that will prepare the returning citizen for reintegration back into society; it's written for the student to gain perspective; and offer guidance to at-risk teens and help fathers become even better men. This book is not intended to be a full scoped intervention model but rather designed based upon a progressive and systemic look at some alternative intervention and proven techniques from a psycho-therapeutic "like" perspective to address some of the social issues from a mental health standpoint.

Purpose and Goal of this book:

- Educate young men and adults on the dynamic of violence and how it affects their lives and their community and how it relates to intergenerational trauma and PTSS.

- Offer a forum to discuss their experiences and challenges as young men and adults.

- Challenge their belief system that perpetuate and controls/dictates their responses and behavior.

- Encourage young men to pursue positive goals and help them develop them.

Target population:

Everyone is encourage to read this book, especially those who have either experience community violence, perpetrated community violence; who have been formally incarcerated or are awaiting trial or are about to be release; or are in a community detention center awaiting parole; community agencies and schools that service young teenagers that are at risk or adults who are experiencing challenges in their lives, all are encourage to read, share and adopt some of the techniques shared in this book.

Philosophy & Function:

I believe that people who are exposed to community violence are at risk of suffering from behavioral and emotional symptoms effecting their development and normal functioning no matter how old they are. This exposure, as some researchers believe, is linked to the high increase of violence in the African American and Hispanic communities. It is through organizations that adopt the techniques of this book and create programs within the community to address some of these issues allow our young men and women who unconsciously suffer from Post-Traumatic Stress Syndrome (PTSS) by being exposed to violence have the opportunity to receive treatment through education and group therapy that challenges their belief systems, attitudes and behavior about violence and serves as a bridge to bring peace within our communities and help educate and address some of the community dysfunctions.

In addition, this book supports a reintegration model for adult males who have been incarcerated or is about to be released from a correctional institution. It is my belief that many young people and adults who desire to do better wish information shared by the writer from his own experience of reintegration was available to help them deal with some of their challenges. This book was intentionally designed with them in mind, to give information to help them structure their lives and make meaning of some of the complex challenges that they cannot understand reintegrating back into a society that is not so welcoming. They say that for returning citizens their chance of re-incarceration is determined within the first 6-months of their release. This is because, for many of them, they do not have a full understanding of what's going on in their lives, and therefore, they react to those external forces (challenges) as threats. These Internal and External forces, which I spoke on in *"Breaking Through: Winning Against the Odds"* are challenges that serve as our "gate keeper". It is up to you to understand those forces that you have control over and for those you don't, you must understand how to navigate them. In this book we will talk about how to deal with some of those internal and external challenges.

[2]

Self-Concept
Why We Must Insist on Using Names

The use of names is a critical component of the *Breaking Through: Changing The Narrative* process. It is essential that you feel comfortable with enforcing the use of your name and not allow anyone to hyphenate, shorten, or change your name with a nickname. Also, you must start using people names that you communicate with, using their personal name when addressing them. It shows mutual respect and gives you and them a sense of identity. Names have power and The Power to Define has been a powerful tool in shaping the mindset of the world. People of power understand the concept of having the power to define. People define the things that have meaning in their life. Whatever delegation they put on an object or person is reflective in the name they associate in describing it, whether they are nouns, pronouns or by-words.

Let's look at marketing for example. I am only using this to show how image reflects a branding that sends a message to society and the world that tells a story about that person (race, character, values, etc.), it says who they are, what they do, their reputation and trustworthiness. Name branding is a powerful tool used in marketing, because the wrong brand can break a company. We tend not to buy a brand that has a negative image or rating. This concept is no different to developing a positive self-image. If a person has a negative self-image or concept of themselves – no one wants to be associated with them. You must change the branding of who you are. Your branding effects many aspects of your life and contributes to many of the disadvantages you find yourselves up against. Rather it be seeking bank loans for businesses, homes, cars or Job placements and opportunities; low interest rates, Etc., there are many stereotypes and negative characteristics that play a part in your branding that makes it more of a challenge for you to succeed. I said 'challenge' to succeeding, not impossible to succeeding. There are cultures all around the world that understands the connection of a name and its attributes to a spiritual connection with the universe. Language contains power, and there is probably nothing in language thought to be more powerful than that of your name. The importance of names has always been ingrained in human spiritual consciousness and has permeated just about every culture around the world from the Far East to Alaska. It's no surprise that expecting parents often

look through baby name books—they want to pick the perfect name for their child. They look not just for the sound of the name, but its associations and the symbolism behind the name. When my child was born, I wanted her name to connect to me and have a spiritual attribute. Her name is *Kendall Adannaya Love Ross*, which her middle name *"Adannaya"* is from the West African Igbo language, and means *"her father's daughter "*, and her first name is a hyphenation of my first and middle name *"Ken Lydell"*. In my family my siblings have names that were passed down the family line and in many cultures it's an honor to be named after an ancestor, or to have someone named after you, and then in other cultures, a new baby name wasn't revealed until the time of the baby's blessing ceremony or 'baby shower', and in cultures with high infant mortality rates, the baby naming was put off until the baby survived to a certain age. This was done to protect the family emotionally, because it kept the baby at an emotional distance in case if the baby died within months after birth.

I usually make it a point to ask young people that I meet what do their name means, especially if their

name is unique. Some people I have met had profound spiritual attributes to their names that connect them to 'their' God or the universe. Yet, what
astounds me is when I asked them about the attributes of their names, nine times out of ten, they give a
clueless look and say something like, "what do you
mean, what do my name means?" or they shrug
their shoulders and say, "I don't know." Another
common response is, "I was told the meaning once,
but I can't remember." Many parents who were
born between 1980 to 2000, who have absorbed or
was influenced by this "common culture" (hip-hop,
self-indulgence and materialism) had decided to
name their children with names that have no cultural identity, and in so doing, have done their child
a dis-service because the name the child holds -
holds no power, no meaning and therefore, no value

and as a result the child tends not to excel to any holistic attributes.

Many people in the African American community neglect the use of their personal name's even if they have a spiritual name. They have adopted "nicknames" or abbreviated their personal name to names that have no positive attributes that leads to a positive self-identity. This neglect is due that our culture seems to take personal names for granted. The most important aspect of personality affected by our names is our *SELF-CONCEPT* of who we are. Our *Self-concept* is developed in us as children, it is "learned" from the verbal and non-verbal messages we receive from people in our environment. Parents are our first message sender but, as we mature and become more and more independent; the messages of our teachers, peers, and society all begin to contribute to us developing a concept of self. In a sense, our self- concept begins to work as a script for the way we act. For example, if a child has an image of themselves as bad or not capable of doing well in school, their be-havior will probably re-flect that image. They will tend to behave the way they think a "bad child" is supposed to be-have, or they will fail to

> *It's amazing how meaning-ful names are, and we don't often even think about it.*

learn as they should even though they may be quite capable of learning and may be very intelligent. They will begin to unconsciously develop the attrib-utes of that name or "nick-name"; it will become a "Self-fulfilled prophecy". That child becomes what they heard all their life: "you're just like your daddy", "sit your stupid ass down", "why you be acting stupid", "you're just a menace to society"; anyone remember that term during the 90's, now its "young thugs", "goons" and "savages". You have all heard some of the negative adjective's parents, teachers and society use to describe our youth and their behavior. Most of us hear these same adjectives and pronouns over and over, day after day. Our society expectation is low of our children succeeding, so many of them now have no standards to meet.

In chapter 2 of my first book *"Breaking Through: Winning Against the Odds",* I talked about how my nickname "Insane" as a teenager affected my behavior while growing up. Once I became conscious of this association I changed my name to a name with positive attributes that helped in my transformation and re-developing of my identity, and in Chapter 2, pages 34-44, I spoke on how movies and music of my generation also helped influences my negative behavior and had an overall negative impact on the moral fabric and culture of our community. (Please read.) When talking with someone and you do not

 know the person name who you are talking to, say "Brother, Sir, Sister, Mr., or Ms., it's im-portant that you use a personal identifica-tion rather than just saying "hey", "you" or "them". The emphasis is that everyone has a name and should be respected as a person. If someone does

not address you correctly, correct them with respect, let them know your name, and share your wishes as to this is how you would like to be address. Immediate and consistent redirection is critical because people often do not hear themselves use pronouns or other objectifying, derogatory language or identifiers. This is intentionally designed to disrupt their flow in speaking and make it more likely that they will slow down and listen to what they are saying.

I realize that this will be an awkward process and you will feel indifferent in cutting people off, but this process is like sports; this is skill development. By practicing proper communication; like the sports athlete, you become better in communicating. Why do athletes do repetitive repetitions of a skill during practice (like shooting baskets, hitting pitches, catching throws) but not in a game? The practice helps develop their concentration, build their comfort level with skills so that during the game they can accomplish their goals. This also helps you to listen carefully and being aware of the subtle objectification and thinks critically before speaking or acting when you interact throughout your community, whether at home, on the job, or interacting with other people in your life.

It is a well-known fact that in order to get people to do things to others that might normally be difficult or counter intuitive, the subject must be delegated to an object: the process of taking away your self-worth and humanity. This tactic was strongly developed and used in wars by the United States government and by other governments around the world while subjugating groups of people through negative stereotypes and war propaganda. It was used during WWII by Germany to dehumanize the Jews by using suggestive negative stereotypes and blaming them for Germany's economical situations. Hitler intent was to use the Jews as a scapegoat to build his political rise on Germany nationalization. It was used by America during the Vietnam War when the U.S. enemies where referred to as "japs, gooks and dinks", and labeling them as "communist" as if the label dehumanizes them; During Slavery to justify the enslavement of Africans. Enslaved Africans names were taken away and replaced with names that had no spiritual connection to their land, language and culture. It was used during reconstruction by the Klu Klux Klan and other groups towards

African American with racist labels as "coons, nig-gers, and savages" that justified their malicious mis-treatment, murdering and continued marginalization and intimidation through "Jim Crow" tactics even to this present day. The negative images perpetuated by America news media sends a message to the world that reinforces these stereo-types of blacks being overly sexual, rapist, murder-ers, lazy, unskilled, uneducated, drug dealers and gang bangers to be feared; killed, and incarcerated.

The results of negative stereotypes imposed on Af-rican Americans by America has caused the African American community psychological damage that has lasted over 400 years. Even now the negative stereotypes (through images, and music) has con-tinued to impart damage and create scares on our community, and as a result we are witnessing the increase of young African Americans being murdered across this country because of self-hate perpetuated by the 'Willie Lynch Syndrome[1] '; mass incarceration and the criminalization of minor acts has led to the increase of African Americans males being incarcerated; negative stereotypes and unclaimed fear has led to "justifiable homicide" by law enforcement across the country of un-armed African Americans. These experience and incidents continues to affect the collective psyche of the African American community because we have absorbed these negative messages and accepted this negative narrative being told by a system design a long time

---

[1] The William Lynch speech is an address purportedly delivered by a certain William Lynch (or Willie Lynch) to an audience on the bank of the James River in Virginia in 1712 regarding control of slaves within the colony. The letter purports to be a verbatim account of a short speech given by a slave owner, in which he tells other slave masters that he has discovered the "secret" to controlling black slaves by setting them against one another.

ago to destroy any black positive movement or 'Black Messiah' leading any movement to up-lift, restore dignity and courage; or to build a strong black united front (*Con-Intel Pro and The King Alfred Plan*)[2] . In *Breaking Through: Winning Against the Odds*, I spoke on the mental health of our community in chapter 9.

---

[2] COINTELPRO (an acronym for COunter INTELligence PROgram) was a series of covert, and at times illegal, projects conducted by the United States Federal Bureau of Investigation (FBI) aimed at surveilling, infiltrating, discrediting, and disrupting domestic political organizations. FBI records show that COINTELPRO resources targeted groups and individuals that the FBI deemed subversive, including anti-Vietnam War organizers, activists of the Civil Rights Movement or Black Power movement (e.g., Martin Luther King, Jr. and the Black Panther Party), feminist organizations, independence movements (such as Puerto Rican independence groups like the Young Lords), and a variety of organizations that were part of the broader New Left.

The King Alfred Plan was a fictional CIA-led scheme supporting an international effort to eliminate people of African descent. Specifically it defined how to deal with the threat of a black uprising in the United States by cordoning off black people into concentration camps in the event of a major racial incident. The Plan first appeared in John A. Williams' 1967 novel, *The Man Who Cried I Am*, an account of the life and death of Richard Wright. In the afterword to later editions, Williams compares the King Alfred Plan to intelligence programs devised by J. Edgar Hoover in the 1960s to monitor the movements of black militants.

[3]

Your Pain Is My Pain
Why we hurt each other

The violence we are witnessing in the African American community perpetuated by young African Americans can be summed up by *Dr. Na'im Akbar* in his introduction in *"Breaking The Chains of Psychological Slavery*, 6Th Ed (2006)

"...the 300-year captivity of Africans in America is an indisputable fact which too many have sought to deny as relevant to anything more than an event of the past. Our formulation suggested that the blemish of these inhumane conditions persists as a kind of post-traumatic stress syndrome on the collective mind of Africans in America and though its original cause cannot be altered, the genesis can be understood. As is accepted in most insight approaches to mental healing (called psychotherapy), a confrontation of the

original trauma and restricting of the mind's faulty adaptation to the assaults can serve to correct these disturbed patterns of responding."

Faced with this reality, it will not be easy *"Changing the Narrative"* and negative behavior exhibited in our young males and now females that have been self-perpetuating for generations as a result of the *"Willie Lynch Syndrome"*, however, being empathetic to the pain and trauma that many of them feel as a result of intergenerational trauma is one of the main techniques I will be using throughout this book to help correct that deteriorating mentality they have adopted as survival/coping mechanism.

The *"Breaking Through"* process is a therapeutic "like" cognitive therapy that addresses PTSD/PTSS because many of us have been exposed to or have experience a traumatic experiences within our life brought on by our current or past environment; upbringing (family dysfunctions); social-economic policies and institutional racism and all the other "ism" that affected the perpetual discrimination towards African-Americans that has keep us as a people marginalized, disenfranchised and separated from participating/competing in mainstream America; which has never been addressed, or, for many of us, we have never received some form of treatment or psychological services to ensure our mental stability. I can use myself as a prime example. I have spent over 23yrs incarcerated in a systemic atmosphere filled with despair and hopelessness absent any positive rehabilitative systems design as treatment to lead to a successful re-entry back into society. If it wasn't from the grace of the Most High God putting people in my life that influenced me and helped shaped my mentality to embraced the concept of growth and development, I would have fallen prey to the same negative influences of my psychological damage. Let me be clear, yes, I still suffer from mental damage as a result of my incarceration, I am just better equipped with masking my hurt, pain and mental suffering better than others due to my level of education and my strong desire to heal myself.

The Chicago Tribune reported that the city of Chicago had 487 homicides and more than 2,800 people shot so far this year. (*Chicago Tribune*, 8/29/2016) This level of violence has become the terrifying norm for many young children and adults, particularly in predominantly black and Latino neighborhoods.

The New York Times had done an interesting chronology of Chicago violence during a Memorial Day weekend in 2016. In their efforts to capture the violence and the pain of those affected, they sent reporters to cover Chicago. Here is one of those stories:

Friday, 10:55 PM

"*Mark Lindsey* is outside his mother's house after a visit. He has chopped off his signature dreadlocks, and a woman has sent him a compliment. He forwards her message to a cousin. It's working already, he writes.

He is behind the wheel of his red Chevy Monte Carlo, a car he so prizes that neighbors see him wash it again and again. A man approaches on foot and opens fire, and *Mr. Lindsey*, 25, is hit. The car lurches forward and strikes a parked pickup truck.

His mother hears the gunfire, runs out and yanks on the locked car door. "Someone get him out of the car!" she shouts over and over.

The screams continue for long minutes. They are jarring here. This section of Ashburn, on the city's Southwest Side, had seemed somewhat removed from the worst of the gun violence. This block on West 75th Place is a cluster of small, neatly edged lawns rolling toward a quiet street where children play soccer. Late at night, television screens glow in living rooms.

"This stuff doesn't happen here," says *Lorenzo Carter*, 28. "We know everybody in this neighborhood."

In only a matter of minutes the police and ambulance will arrive, but the mother is frantic. "What's taking so long?" she shouts.

Witnesses see *Mr. Lindsey* in the driver's seat, his head resting against the window. He is taken to Advocate Christ Medical Center and is pronounced dead at 11:34 p.m.

Mr. Lindsey worked at a railroad management company, friends say. "He was one of the success stories," says *Leroy Cook*, 26.

The police have made no arrests in the case, and a motive is uncertain. *Mr. Lindsey* was arrested just a day before on a domestic battery charge. He was released on bond.

Neighbors say the shooting shows that the violence is trickling onto blocks that had long been considered safe.

"Shooting in Chicago is like a cancer," says *Charles Parker*, 46, standing on the street with another neighbor. "It's starting to spread out, and I just figured it was a matter of time." (*This article was by Monica Davey-New York Times* (2016)

This is only one such story of what the families and the people of the community must deal with, and to begin to understand what motivates such behaviors,

we must understand the generic roots[3] of the behavior in order to implement effective prevention;
one must begin to understand the many reasons for
bad decisions made by individuals which are tied up
in understanding the psychology of group self-
motivation.

Dr. Joy DeGruy Leary, who teaches social justice, has
developed a theory from over 12 years of research
that explain how both overt and subtle forms of racism have damaged the collective African American
psyche which manifested through poor mental and
physical health, family and relationship dysfunction,
and self-destructive impulses. *Dr. Leary* states that

---

[3] To understand the core problems with behavior in the African American community, we must understand it from using a "Root Cause Analysis Approach" (RCA). This approach requires us to use scientific methodologies. One such methodology is *Events and Casual Factor Analysis*. Looking at this problem of behavior from a macro-level and looking at the shift and timeline of the change in behavior we, can then understand the core root causes of what is happening in the black community.

African Americans today suffer from a particular kind of intergenerational trauma: Post Traumatic Slave Syndrome (PTSS).

'When African Americans accept the deprecating accounts and images portrayed by the media, literature, music and the arts as a true mirror of themselves, we are actually allowing ourselves to be socialized by a racist society. Evidence of racist socialization can be readily seen when African American children limit their aspirations' It can be seen when we use the accumulation of material things as the measure of self-worth and success.

So, in spite of all our forbears who worked to survive and gain their freedom; in spite of the efforts of all those who fought for civil rights' we are continually being socialized by this society to undervalue ourselves, to undermine our own efforts and, ultimately, to hate ourselves. We are raising our children only to watch America tear them down. Today, the legacy of slavery remains etched in our souls. Understanding the role our past plays in our present attitudes, outlooks, mindsets and circumstances is important if we are to free ourselves from the spiritual, mental and emotional shackles that bind us today, shackles that limit what we believe we can be, do and have. Understanding the role Post-Traumatic Slave Syndrome plays in our evolution may be the key that helps to set us on the path to well-being.' (Post Traumatic Slave Syndrome, Chapter 5, Slavery's Children)

I truly believe that understanding PTSS and working from a therapeutic foundation to deliver services is key to bringing real solutions to the problems many African Americans are dealing with internally. It is only rational to believe people past affect their future and by ignoring it doesn't make it go away.

Social Scientists all around the world have one core belief, they all believe in a cause-and-effect world. They are obsessed with describing those causes, and then measuring and predicting the consequential effects. Public Health professionals seek to understand cause and effects by measuring the strength of the associations, and determine which causes are detrimental to the public health. If those causes are amenable to change, their logical solution and reaction would be to devise intervention strategies that would reduce the adverse health risk. We have witness this over and over in the public health field.

Public health official would monitor the morbidity and the mortality outcomes that include risk factors associated with causality and then they will use this information to predict outcomes and prescribe their diagnoses/theory which would affect public policies. Such as in the case of health risk associated to smoking, alcohol use, obesity, heart disease, or how the lack of exercise affects one's health. However, social scientist surveillance on the risk factors associated to high levels of poverty, drug abuse and crime in the African American community relative to intergenerational trauma has been silent; they have rejected the theory proposed by *Dr. Leary* and others on PTSS, or if commentary was added in attempt to address the association it lacked a method of measuring the generic events that are, in turn, associated with such risk factors, such as, the antagonistic relationship between the African American community and the police force, they blame it on the community bad relationship and unwillingness to submit to authority; mass incarceration of African Americans is blamed on their violent tendencies or propensity to commit crimes; the proliferation of guns and drugs in the African American community that escalates the violence is blamed on social conditions created by themselves; high unemployment in the African American community is blamed on their own lack of unwillingness to work; they blame the victim for their victimization dismissing all the overwhelming evidence of racism, bigotry, and discriminatory laws and public policies.

B.F. Skinner developed a theory of *"Selection by Consequences"*, *Skinner* describes this theory as *"what we call behavior evolved as a set of functions furthering between organism and environments"* *(Skinner, 1984, p. 477)* this theory 'in my understanding' is

equivalent to his theory on *"operant conditioning"*. People respond and develop according to the stimuli they receive from their environments. People are a product of their environment in other words. Skinner further developed a three-level tier of understanding behavioral evolution that is critical to the *"selection by consequences"* theory. The first level, Level-1 according to Skinner is governed by biology. This level of selection is driven by the need to "survive". Everyone has this instinctive nature of wanting to survive. People in the African American community has limited options, and many feels that society has abandon them and have created systems to keep them marginalized were they are unable to fulfill their dreams or reach for that proverbial plateau of freedom and liberty that their counterparts of other nationalities have had the pleasure of experiencing and benefiting from. (see *Breaking Through: Winning Against the Odds, Chapter 3, Locus of Control pg 45-55*)

The national unemployment rate among African American's is much higher than the unemployment rate for whites. African American's unemployment rate is 9.5 percent compared to 4.5 percent among whites. This gap is largely due to the disparity in education. Accordingly, to *Valarie Wilson*, a researcher from the *Economic Policy Institute* (EPI), African Americans only represent 22 percent of the population with College degrees, compared to 41 percent of whites. Wilson looked at the census data and determined that "the unemployment rate is higher among those who didn't attend college. Among those who hadn't completed high school, whites had an unemployment rate of 6.9 percent. But for African Americans, the situation was much more extreme: Their unemployment rate was almost two-and-a-half times higher, at 16.6 percent.

And a gap persists even among those who have completed a bachelor's degree or higher, with an unemployment rate of 4.1 percent for African Americans compared to 2.4 percent for white Americans with the same degree." (*The Atlantic* 12/5/2015)

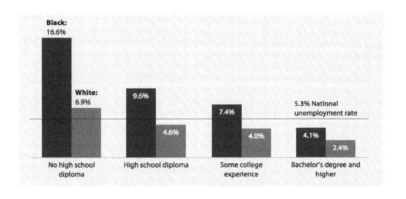

Even though this article does not talk about the other factors that contribute to the high unemployment rate among African Americans; such as the institutional racism, the article does point out, that despite blacks and whites having a comparable degree the unemployment rate is extremely higher for blacks with the same degree. Mixing these two factors in an over-populated environment with limited resources brings the high potential for violence and adds to the belief that the "system is against me" mentality.

However, the need for *"self-actualization"* described in *Maslow's Hierarchy of Needs*[4] (1943) do not dissolve because of these external factors. What had happened, and what had evolved was that the marginalized has stopped trying to integrate into a "system" that they were kept out of. They have witnessed their parents sitting on the "sidelines"

---

[4] Maslow's basic position is that as one becomes more <u>self-actualized;</u> more wise (develops wisdom) and automatically knows what to do in a wide variety of situations. Maslow's hierarchy of needs explains why each of us is motivated by needs. Our most basic needs are inborn, having evolved over tens of thousands of years. Abraham Maslow's Hierarchy of Needs helps to explain how these needs motivate us all. Maslow's Hierarchy of Needs states that we must satisfy each need in turn, starting with the first, which deals with the most obvious needs for survival itself. Only when the lower order needs of physical and emotional well-being are satisfied are we concerned with the higher order needs of influence and personal development. Conversely, if the things that satisfy our lower order needs are swept away, we are no longer concerned about the maintenance of our higher order needs. Maslow's original Hierarchy of Needs model was developed between 1943-1954, and first widely published in Motivation and Personality in 1954.

and have heard stories of their grandparents experiencing physical racism and discrimination, and now they are experiencing systemic institutional racism themselves. They have decided to perpetuate their livelihood through 'whatever means necessary' an since they can only operate within boundaries; they tend to make victims of the victimized and opt out of the system and abandon the civil rights agenda of integration. They adopted and adapted traits that they felt was necessary for their survival and that innate desire to survive - dissipated or were no longer an option for them. They begin to live their lives recklessly by any means necessary.

I look forward to developing a conceptual workable lesson around *Maslow's Hierarchy of Needs* to help re-design how we seek to fulfill our needs absent external support.

The second level of *B.F. Skinner's "Selection by Consequence"*, Level-2 is governed by *psychology*. This level of selection is concern with the individual development of behavior. This level is critical in understanding the behavior we are witnessing in the

African American community. The psychology of individual behavior is adjusted to deal with a hostile environment. In *Breaking Through: Winning Against the Odds*, I mention how my prison environment was only designed to punish and through the isolation of incarceration, living in a harsh prison environment it is so easily to begin to adapt to the institutional social norms. Which some would describe the behavior as becoming institutionalized; I would say it was a progressive way of losing your humanity, yet, adapting to survive in a harsh environment. Which prison is only a microcosm of society, you adapt in order to survive in a hostile world. Evolution has taught us that organism adept to their environment - from the evolution of changing physical characteristics in man and animal, to the "survival of the fittest". Even though *Skinner* suggested that the environment should not influence the individual. It's inevitable. The influences of the social forces are strong and only a few are able to escape the grips of those internal and external influences that draw many young people in. Therefore, this book is critical; because it offers psychotherapeutic & cognitive behavioral "like" counseling through education and the sharing of information design to challenge and change the behavior.

Level-3 of *"Selection by Consequence"* is governed by *anthropology* and is concerned with evolution of societal behavior. Skinner believed that the group (community) should dictate the behavior (trait) as the result of circumstances, rather than letting the circumstances dictate the behavior. I agree whole heartily, yet, because the African American community is so split on social issues there is no common leadership to address the oppression of the African American community; there is no national agenda, no national leaders to address African American's grievances. The establish and elected leadership has compromised their integrity and is not trusted among the younger generation to represent them, nor, is there any national institutions of higher learning that produce an afro-centric curriculum that promotes cultural values and social responsibilities that the body as a whole (the black community) has solely adopted. For a long time, churches have been the only stable institution within the black community, like Trinity United Church of Christ on Chicago far south side which was founded on the revolutionary spirit of Jesus Christ led by Dr. Rev. Jeremiah A. Wright (ret.) now lead by Otis Moss III, which was built on the mission of changing the conditions of the people in the community in which the church is built and the people they serve. However, there are many churches that have lost their way to this new age religion of prosperity preaching, they lack the revolutionary rhetoric towards building strong self-sufficient communities independent of any social hand-outs. The church has now crippled the black community by continuing leading us into the hands of the powers that be, by emphasizing that our salvation shall come from the sky. The spirituality of the black church is now absent any strong support from black males that represent the vanguard/strength of our community. It would make a great discussion to find out why the black churches no longer appeal to this younger black male population.

It is of my opinion - that the civil rights generation were only concerned with the *"talent tenth"*[5] for so long that, as a result the younger generation was abandon and their voices were ignored for decades - until recently over the last few years the *'Black Lives Matter'* movement became relevant, it was born out of necessity and frustration; the ingredients of all movements and revolutions, such as the Black Power Movement of the 60's & 70's. These voices represented the victims of community violence either from among their own peers or from law enforcement. The founders of the 'Black Lives Movement' fought for legitimacy, and to have a platform to express their grievances and bring attention to the

---

[5] The Talented Tenth is a phrase made popular by Du Bois in an article published in *The Negro Problem* in 1903. He believed that all efforts should be focus on elevating the privilege and best minds, and most educated ones of the black community, which was opposed to Booker T. Washington industrial and technical school movement.

plight of their generation. They had their challenges of not being accepted by the old vanguard generation, or new religious leadership of the black community who refuse to allow them a seat at the table; They was complicit and joined the conspiracy with mainstream media and white America in the villainization and in the discrediting of the 'Black Lives Movement' as not being a legitimate movement to silence their voices, because they were not lead by the *'Jessie Jackson's* or the *Al Sharpton's* or any other member of the black appointed leadership. This fragmentation of leadership within the black community has for far too long diminishes the channeling of transcending community values and moral principles to the next generation and as a direct result contributed to the perpetuation of intergenerational trauma.

One distinctive difference I have learned by looking at my prison experience is that, when comparing society and prison, each has its own ecosystem. In prison our ecosystem was only a microcosm and reflection of the society we was exiled from, we had our own set of rules for correctional staff to prisoners, and from my point of view in my comparison to *Skinners* Level-3 *of Selection by Consequence* is that after spending all those years incarcerated, those rules we lived by govern our code of conduct and establish what was acceptable levels of respect and acceptable behavior. In those small isolated communities (prisons) we seen how the influence of respectable leadership can affect the larger community, which transcended the walls of the prison socio-cultural ecosystem despite of the different races and religious affiliations, we understood that we had a common core interest that were similar in nature and therefore made us more peers than strangers, so our commonality inspire our unity to some degree because if the outcome is achieved then we all benefited either directly or in some secondary or tertiary degree. I speak from the references of my own experience and how those grassroots leaders like *Larry Hoover* created a system of transcending values and moral conduct to the larger society from behind prison walls. Their voices echoing from those tiny ecosystems to a larger society came with a cry of urgency and moral conviction, unlike the voices of these "establishment appointed leaders of the black community" who voices of change was "slow and grudging" but, change from the inside-out could be observed as swift and embraced more easily.

Larry Hover (1977)

[4]

Intergenerational Trauma
Our Pain/Our Suffering

D*r. Joy DeGruy Leary,* term the theory of PTSS to help explain the consequences of multigenerational oppression from centuries of chattel slavery and institutionalized racism, and to identify the resulting maladaptive behaviors she turned her study into the ground-breaking book *Post Traumatic Slave Syndrome: America's Legacy of Enduring Injury and Healing,* published in 2005. Researchers have long investigated how historical trauma is passed down through generations, and findings suggest that actual memories are transmitted through the DNA, research conducted and documented from Jews, Native Americans and other groups support this finding which is acknowledge by other social anthropologist and psychologist. If this is so, that same concept and diagnosis can be applied to the impact of slavery on African Americans.

Post Traumatic Slave Syndrome (PTSS) differs from *Post-Traumatic Stress Disorder* (PTSD). PTSD results from a *single* trauma experienced directly or indirectly. *Dr. Joy DeGruy Leary* writes, *"When we look at American chattel slavery, we are not talking about a single trauma; we're talking about multiple traumas over lifetimes and over generations,"* and *"Living in Black skin is a whole other level of stress."* In formulating her theory, she wondered: *"What happens when stressed people lack treatment for generations?*

How have Black people coped? What maladaptive behaviors have we invented—now misinterpreted as "cultural"—to survive in a toxic environment? "How do we phase out, as a people, that which is harmful that which builds resilience and that which is absolutely pathological?" asks *DeGruy,* because figuring that out is essential if we are to break the cycle. *"We have to learn to not pass along the broken material. We have to learn how to keep ourselves safe."*

The clinical information shared in this book is specifically designed to address these questions posed *by Dr. DeGruy* on the social-psychological issues affecting many young men and women in our community and specifically African Americans children and adults.

While in school pursuing my counseling degree, I learned about this case study on traumatic transmission or shared psychosis. Even though the case in discussion is relative to a patient who suffered from delusional thinking and hallucinations, the correlation is about the substance of how pain, anger and psychological trauma are transferred through generations; not to say African Americans trauma is based upon delusional and hallucinated claims, our pain is real, history is real and it should never be forgotten, as many would want us to forget it or 'white-wash' it, or prevent it from being told, learned or taught in schools.

This case study was rooted on trying to understand a child delusional thinking. After looking at the family history, it was discovered that the child's mother was diagnosed with schizophrenia and use to always warn her child that there where monsters in the basement. The child grew up hearing this for years and soon she begins to believe that there were monsters in the basement. Over the years the mother's fears transferred to the child. So, the child grew up thinking that there were monsters in the basement and would suffer the same psychological reactions of fear and anxiety as her mother would. *In Breaking Through: Winning Against the Odds*, I spoke on how the African American community suffers from a shared psychosis as a result of intergenerational trauma brought on by PTSS. (*Breaking Through: Winning Against the Odds - Your Mental Health*, chapter 9, page 104)

Intergenerational trauma was first discussed during the 1960's among psychologist concerning the transmission of trauma from holocaust survivors to second and third generations[6].

Intergenerational trauma is defined as trauma that is transferred from the first generation of trauma survivors to the second and further generations of offspring of the survivors via complex post-traumatic stress disorder mechanisms.

---

[6] Transgenerational trauma is trauma that is transferred from the first generation of trauma survivors to the second and further generations of offspring of the survivors via complex post-traumatic stress disorder mechanisms. The so-called *concentration camp syndrome* (also known as survivor syndrome) appeared; clinicians observed in 1966 that large numbers of children of Holocaust survivors were seeking treatment in clinics in Canada. The grandchildren of Holocaust survivors were overrepresented by 300% among the referrals to a child psychiatry clinic in comparison with their representation in the general population. The phenomenon of children of traumatized parents being affected directly or indirectly by their parents' post-traumatic symptoms has been described by some authors as *secondary traumatization* (in reference to the *second generation*). To include the *third generation*, as well, the term intergenerational transmission of trauma was introduced. (Fossion, P., Rejas, M., Servais, L., Pelc, I. & Hirsch, S. (2003). "Family approach with grandchildren of Holocaust survivors," *American Journal of Psychotherapy*, 57(4), 519-527).

Complex post-traumatic stress disorders (C-PTSD) is a proposed diagnostic term for a set of symptoms resulting from prolonged stress of a social and/or interpersonal nature, especially in the context of interpersonal dependence (in this case - the African American relationship with America). This diagnosis is not yet recognized in the *Diagnostic and Statistical Book of Mental Disorders* (DSM-V) yet many journals have been published in regard to complex trauma. *Judith Herman* first discussed C-PTSD in 1992 in her book *Trauma & Recovery. (Judith L. Herman (May 30, 1997, Trauma and Recovery: The Aftermath of Violence –From Domestic Abuse to Political Terror.*) In a sense, the African American community relationship with America is like a domestic abuse relationship described by *Judith Herman*, with the African American community being the victim of abuse and just like any classic case of the *"cycles of violence"*, we return to our abuser and justify their abuse and forget the abuse ever happen, we return back to the "honeymoon stage" because of our dependent relationship.

The term complex trauma describes *"both exposure to multiple traumatic events, often of an invasive, interpersonal nature and describes the wide-ranging, long-term impact (intergenerational) of this exposure."*

The events described earlier concerning community violence and intergenerational trauma's (slavery, racism, and Jim Crowism) are severe and pervasive experiences that exposed children and adults to traumatic events in life and the resulting impact are now disrupting a whole community development and the very foundation/ formation of a positive self-image/self-esteem of themselves internally and reflective externally (negative images of African Americans) throughout the world.

This subject of intergenerational transmission of trauma is not an ellucid conversation that can be explained in simple terms. However, awareness of the transmission of the intergenerational processes will inhibit the continual transmission of the pathologies to succeeding generations.

Traumatic events affect individuals, families, communities and society in many different direct and indirect ways. The strong opposition to the PTSS theory being applied to the African American situation and current conditions is that history has nullified the effects of slavery on the current generation.

I strongly disagree, as stated in studies applied to other nationalities, those studies have shown that intergenerational trauma transcends multigeneration, especially if the trauma is continuously repeated over and over and over in one form or another, so, if the diagnosis applies to them, why not African Americans? I am going to leave that question for you to figure out.

However, let's just briefly look at the African American historical timeline of repeated oppression.

Historical Timeline to PTSS/Intergenerational Trauma

Beginning with slavery in America; even though I hate to start African American history at this point, however for clarity of intergenerational trauma and highlighting the timeline of our experiences, I must start here. From the beginning of slavery here in America starting during the late 1600s with the raping, murdering, beatings and separation of families. No other nationality or ethnic group ever endure or experience this form of treatment and trauma. The African American community still experiencing the residual effects of this trauma from over 400 years; the struggles against oppression, lynching and beatings: *The Slave Codes* 1705; *The Fugitive Slave Act of* 1793; *The Black Codes of* 1865-1870's; *Jim Crow Laws* and *Segregation*; *Three Strikes Laws*; *War on Drugs/crime Policies of the* 1990's. Laws and social policies designed to oppress and marginalize a group of people based upon their skin color and national origin. Policies that have had long lasting lingering effects of trauma that is still present unto this day. Social policies that lead to thousands of murders by lynching's; burning of whole towns and communities; confiscation of land and businesses; forced servitude through passing of laws after slavery was abolished through the 13 amendment; divestment in black communities. There is a long list of acts committed with the endorsement of the American government that has contributed to the transmission of the trauma we are discussing.

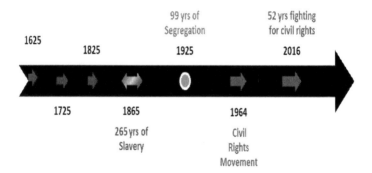

Awareness of this timeline can help you better understand and put things in perspectives relative to our struggles and challenges here in America. This timeline and discussion is not only for the layman, but service providers as well. Because one of the *"Core Competencies"* of being and effective counselor, facilitator or community service provider and in building relational bridges that engender trust and confidence is having sensitivity to the cultural and personal perspective of your clients that leads to a genuine empathy, humility, respect and acceptance of your client's cultural belief system that was developed by their experiences.

We cannot ignore or disregard the frustration and suffering of the community in which we are sent to serve. We must consider their culture, history and their individual 'back' stories and help them put it in perspective to find solutions, answers and a sense of direction that they can function within.

Cotton fields of Mississippi

Africans capture for the slave trade

Public beatings of African Americans

Public lynching and torture of African Americans

Mechanical measures imposed on slaves to prevent escape

The Fugitive Slave Bill that prevented the helping or harboring of runaway slave (1854)

36

By the revised code, *seventy-one* offences are punished with *Death* when committed by slaves, and by nothing more than imprisonment when by the whites. *Stroud's Sketch,* p. 107.

Rev. Code. In the trial of slaves, the court consists of five justices without juries, even in capital cases. L p. 420.

MARYLAND.—*Stat. Law, Sec. 8.* Any slave for rambling in the night or riding horses by day without leave, or running away, may be punished by whipping, cropping or branding in the cheek, or otherwise, not rendering him unfit for labour p. 237.

Any slave convicted of petty treason, murder, or *wilful burning of dwelling houses,* may be *sentenced to have the right hand cut off, to be hanged in the usual manner, the head severed from the body, the body divided into four quarters, and the head and quarters set up in the most public place in the country where such fact was committed !!* p. 190.

Act 1717, chap. 13, Sec. 5. Provides that any free coloured person marrying a slave, becomes a slave for life, except mulattoes born of white women.

DELAWARE.—*Laws.* More than six men slaves, meeting together, not belonging to one master, unless on lawful business of their owners, may be whipped to the extent of 21 lashes each. p. 104.

UNITED STATES.—*Constitution.* The chief pro-slavery provisions of the constitution, as is generally known, are 1st. that by virtue of which the slave States are represented in Congress for three-fifths of their slaves ;* 2nd. that requiring the giving up of any run away slaves to their masters; 3rd. that pledging the physical force of the whole country to suppress insurrections, i. e. attempts to gain freedom by such means as the framers of the instrument themselves used.

Act of Feb. 12, 1793. Provides that any master or his agent may seize any person whom he claims as a "fugitive from service," and take him before a judge of U. S. court, or magistrate of the city or county where he is taken, and the magistrate, on proof, in support of the claim, to his satisfaction, must give the claimant a certificate authorizing the removal of such fugitive to the state he fled from.†

DISTRICT OF COLUMBIA.—The act of Congress incorporating Washington city, gives the corporation power to prescribe the terms and conditions on which free negroes and mulattoes may reside in the city. *City Laws,* 6 and 11. By this authority, the city in 1827 enacted that any free coloured person coming there to reside, should give the Mayor satisfactory evidence of his freedom, and enter into bond with two free hold sureties, in the sum of five hundred dollars, for his good conduct, to be renewed each year for three years; or failing to do so, must leave the city, or be committed to the work house, for not more than one year, and if he still refuse to go, may be again committed for the same period, and so on. *Ib* 198.

Coloured persons residing in the city, who cannot prove their title to freedom, shall be imprisoned as absconding slaves. *Ib.* 198.

Coloured persons found without free papers may be arrested as runaway slaves, and after two month's notice, if no claimant appears, must be advertised ten days, and sold to pay their jail fees.‡ *Stroud,* 85, note.

The city of Washington grants a license, to *trade in slaves,* for profit, as agent or otherwise, for four hundred dollars. *City Laws,* p. 249.

---

* By the operation of this provision, twelve slave holding states, whose white population only equals that of New York and Ohio, send to Congress 24 senators and 102 representatives, while these two states only send 4 senators and 59 representatives.

† Thus it may be seen that a man may be doomed to slavery by an authority not considered sufficient to settle a claim of *twenty dollars.*

‡ The prisons of the district, built with the money of the nation, are used as store houses of the slaveholders' human merchandize. " From the statement of a keeper of a jail in Washington, it appears that in five years, upwards of 450 coloured persons were committed in the national prison in that city, for safe keeping ; i. e., until they could be disposed of in the course of the *slave trade,* besides nearly 300 who had been taken up as runaways." *Miner's speech in H. Rep. in* 1829.

Reader, you uphold these laws *while you do nothing for their repeal.* You can do much. You can take and read the anti-slavery journals. They will give you an impartial history of the cause, and arguments with which to convert its enemies. You can countenance and aid those who are labouring for its promotion. You can petition against slavery ; can refuse to vote for slaveholders or pro-slavery men, constitutions and compacts ; can abstain from products of slave labour ; and can use your social influence to spread right principles and awaken a right feeling. Be as earnest for freedom as its foes are for slavery, and you can diffuse an anti-slavery sentiment through your whole neighbourhood, and merit " the blessing of them that are ready to perish."

The ANTI-SLAVERY BUGLE is published every Friday at Salem, Columbiana County, Ohio, Price $1.50 in advance. Benjamin S. Jones and J. Elizabeth Hitchcock, Editors; Jas. Barnaby, Jr., General Agent.

Copies of this tract can be had *gratis,* by applying at the office of the Bugle. Subscriptions to National A. S. Standard, Liberator, Pennsylvania Freeman, and Herald of Freedom, received at the same place.

Newspaper article on Tulsa Oklahoma Bombing (1921)

Tulsa black residents' homes bombed and set on fire (1921)

Civil right marchers attacked by Selma Police force, what was described as "bloody Monday". (1965)

Dr. Martin Luther King Jr.

Civil Rights Marchers attacked by Dogs

Civil rights marchers hosed and beaten

Civil Rights marchers hosed

Fred Hampton

Black Panther Marchers

Black Panther Party members targeted by FBI and local law enforcement

Panther Clark Expected Death,

A Tribune reporter interviewed friends, acquaintances, and relatives of two members of the Black Panther party slain in a raid by state's attorney's police Dec. 4 in an effort to give an in-depth view of their lives. Today's story is on Mark Clark, who was chairman of the party's Peoria chapter.

BY JOSEPH BOYCE

"A slave of natural death who dies
Can't balance out two dead foes,
I'd rather be without the shame,
A bullet lodged within my brain.
If I were not to reach our goal,
Let bleeding cancer torment my soul."

This was the favorite poem of Mark Clark, 22, slain Black Panther party leader, according to his sister, Eleanor, 20.

Its originator was Alprentice [Bunchy] Carter, Panther defense minister who was shot to death Jan. 17 during a meeting of 150 black students in the University of California, Los Angeles.

Killed in Police Raid

Clark, chairman of the party's Peoria chapter, was fatally shot by state's attorney's police Dec. 4 in a raid on an apartment at 2337 Monroe st. Fred Hampton, 21, state party chairman, also was killed.

Clark and another Peoria Panther, Anthony [Tony] Harris, 21, had come to Chicago Nov. 20 to confer with party leaders about sharing up the Peoria chapter which was failing because of a "lack of support," Eleanor Clark said.

Harris was arrested Dec. 2 after a gun battle with police in a building at 6059-69 Merrill av. He was charged with attempted murder and aggravated battery.

This leaves Peoria with only one "active" Panther party member, Eleanor Clark said.

Impressed by Activity

"He said to me then that the Panthers were really doing something in California—something worthwhile. This was before anything had started here."

Mark became active in the party after a family friend, a Panther member, came from California to Peoria for a visit, his sister said. "They talked, and the friend gave Mark some literature to read and Mark decided he wanted to join," she said.

"He was the first member here. Other friends joined but some quit, some were not very active, and others didn't participate. Most were in the training stage," Eleanor Clark said.

A Thinker, Friend Says

"Mark was a thinker first and foremost," a Peoria friend, Moses Hardy, 23, said of Clark.

"He wanted to do something far and above being a member of the Black Panther party. He had a feeling for people and placed them before himself," Hardy said.

Mark Clark was born June 28, 1947, in St. Francis hospital, Peoria, the ninth of 17 children of William and Fannie Clark. William Clark was pastor of Holy Temple Church of God in Christ and worked in the foundry at the Caterpillar company for 28 years. He died last May.

Mother in Michigan

Mrs. Fannie Clark spent most of her time as a housewife but at one time worked in St. Fran-

cis hospital and occasionally did domestic work. She and some of the Clark children now live in Flint, Mich.

Mark went to Lincoln elementary school from 1st thru 6th grade and then attended Roosevelt Junior High school.

"He liked the process of learning, but he didn't like school. Most of his knowledge came from his own efforts," his sister said.

"He read a lot and a variety of materials. He became interested in the life of man and was especially fascinated by Darwin's theory of evolution — the relationship of man to other species," she said.

Flair for the Drama

Mark, who was only a fair student, but who excelled in subjects that interested him, displayed a great talent for art, drama, and speech, Eleanor Clark said.

"At the age of 4, he was the youngest person ever to be a member of the Craver Players," a local acting company, she said.

When she and Mark were in their early teens they were invited to become members of

the Peoria Players, the city's most prestigious drama group, she said.

"But he didn't think seriously about it. They had such limited parts and he was determined not to go on stage carrying a tray."

"Always Adventurous"

"When he was young, he didn't aspire to the things that most kids do, like eventually becoming a doctor or lawyer. He was always adventurous," Eleanor Clark said.

"I think he finally found what he wanted to do. He didn't accept things as is. He was a nonconformist. He was the type of person who, regardless of whether anyone went along with his ideas, it didn't make any difference. He was going to do what he thought was right and appropriate," she said.

"I remember when we were kids and used to watch stories about the cowboys and Indians on television that he used to tell me all that stuff was a lie.

Admirer of Geronimo

"He used to say the reason the Indians were on reservations was because they were too proud to be slaves. He admired Geronimo because he refused to accept the reservation, or peonage — slavery," Eleanor Clark said.

"This was when he was a child. He was very sensitive to others' feelings."

Her brother got along well with people even tho he wasn't an extrovert, she said.

After Mark finished at Roosevelt he went to Manual High school but did not graduate, his sister said.

While at Manual, Mark had disciplinary problems including one in which he allegedly assaulted a teacher.

"The school has a majority

Mark Clark

8-14—THE SUN   Friday, Dec. 5, 1969

Black Panther Leader Slain

Fred Hampton, leader of the Black Panther party in Illinois, was one of two killed in a gun fight with police yesterday in Chicago. Hampton is shown as he addressed a protest rally outside Chicago Courthouse last October. At right is famed baby Doctor Benjamin Spock.

Chicago Policemen Kill Two Black Panthers in Gun Fight

CHICAGO (UPI)—Black Panthers and police fought a 15-minute gun battle Thursday when police raided a Panther stronghold to search for weapons. Two Black Panthers, including the party's Illinois chairman, were killed and four were wounded.

Two members of the state's attorney's police force were wounded—neither seriously—in the gunfight on Chicago's West Side.

The dead were Fred Hampton, 22, head of the party in Illinois, and Mark Clark, 22, Peoria, Ill., reputed downstate leader of the black militant organization.

Three persons, one a girl said to be about eight months pregnant, were taken into custody by police at the scene— an apartment on West Monroe Street about one-half block from the Black Panther headquarters.

State's Attorney Edward V. Hanrahan said police seized seven pistols and revolvers, six shotguns and one .303 caliber rifle. One of the shotguns had been stolen from a police vehicle, police said. Hanrahan said the raid also netted about 1,000 rounds of ammunition.

Fourteen police went to the

MARK CLARK
· · · one of two killed

apartment shortly before 5 a.m. after receiving reports from informers that sawed-off shotguns and other illegal weapons were cached there. They were armed with a search warrant signed by Criminal Court Judge Robert Collins.

Sgt. Dan Groth, who led the raid, said he knocked on the door and received the response. "Who's there?" He said he identified himself as a police officer.

When repeated knocks brought no further response, he said, he forced open the door with his shoulder and entered the darkened apartment.

Police said a woman lying in bed in the living room opened fire on them with a shotgun and they returned the fire. Then "eight or nine individuals began firing with carbines, shotguns and handguns," police said.

Groth said he several times "asked all gunfire to stop and asked everyone to throw up their hands and lay down their ammunition." Each time a voice from the back room shouted, "Shoot it out," he said.

Finally all the Black Panthers surrendered. Hampton's body was found in a rear bedroom, a .45 caliber pistol in his hand and a shotgun by his side, police said.

Hospital attendants said two of the wounded Black Panthers — Ronald Satchel, 19, Panther minister of medicine, and Blair Anderson, 18—were in serious condition. Satchel suffered four wounds, Anderson two.

FBI targeted assassination of Fred Hampton and Mark Clark, December 4, 1969.

Malcom X targeted assassination February 21, 1965

Dr. Martin Luther King Jr. assassinated April 4, 1968

From slaves to prisoners, the criminalization of African Americans

Lifetime Likelihood of Imprisonment

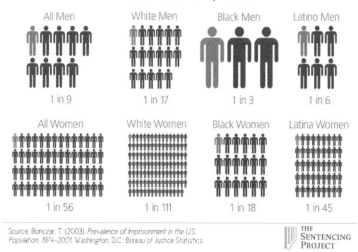

All Men	White Men	Black Men	Latino Men
1 in 9	1 in 17	1 in 3	1 in 6

All Women	White Women	Black Women	Latina Women
1 in 56	1 in 111	1 in 18	1 in 45

Source: Bonczar, T. (2003). *Prevalence of Imprisonment in the U.S. Population 1974–2001.* Washington, D.C.: Bureau of Justice Statistics

THE
SENTENCING
PROJECT

[5]

Empathic Listening
Listening to Understand

Being an epithetic listener as author *Stephen R. Covey* describe it, "involves a very deep shift in paradigm." It's not just the active listening to a person then regurgitating what the person said, nor is it the "yeah, Uh-huh, Right". As a friends, teachers, counselors or facilitators you MUST listen to understand. Empathic Listening rule # 1 is "seek first to understand, then to be understood." Our shortcoming as facilitator, counselors, and or friends is that we have a tendency to give advice to solve "their" problems. Rather than diagnosing the problem, take the time to deeply understand the root of the problem.

Author *Stephen R. Covey* states that "Most people do not listen with the intent to understand; they listen with the intent to reply. They're either speaking or preparing to speak. They're filtering everything through their own paradigms, reading their autobiography into other people's lives."

Empathetic Listening is a technique which can help you manage your own *cognitive biases*. What are *cognitive Biases*? We all have them; these are our different listening filters. These filters distort or ability to effectively listen — the idea that we all have preconceived ideas about who we're communicating with (our stereotypes and judgments) prevents us from being fair and objective. Overcoming that Listening Bias is crucial to becoming a better listener and communicator. And the first step, to paraphrase the old cliché, is recognizing that the problem exists. Once we see in ourselves where our predispositions lie, we can much more easily take steps to not let that bias influence our mindset as we communicate. We can ask questions, start a dialog, look for clarity, and focus objectively on the topic being discussed and be in a better position to help someone.

There are four main biases that we filter through as humans that affect our listening skills:

1. The *confirmation bias* refers to our tendency to seek evidence that supports our current views. People naturally want reassurance that their views are correct. They don't typically challenge their own

views by seeking evidence to disprove them. It's threatening to people's sense of who they are to admit when they're wrong. This threat makes the *confirmation bias* one of the most potent cognitive biases because most people don't actively look for evidence that their views might be wrong and will sometimes reject new information contrary to their belief. *Franz Fanon* talks about *cognitive dissonance* in his book *"Black Skin, White Masks"* (1952), he states:

"sometimes people hold a core belief that is very strong. When they are presented with evidence that works against that belief, the new evidence cannot be accepted. It would create a feeling that is extremely uncomfortable, called cognitive dissonance, and because it is so important to protect the core belief, they will rationalize, ignore and even deny anything that doesn't fit in with the core belief."

In *Fanon's "Black Skin White Masks"* he analyzed from a psychological perspective the cultural effects of Africans assimilating in a French dominated culture. This cultural assimilation greatly affected the black man's ability to balance his cultural reality being Algerian and living French, similar to African Americans cultural struggles after post-civil rights and Jim Crowism. Here we are confronted with a dual situation of *Confirmation Biasness* and *Cognitive Dissonance*. As a black man who faced discrimination and the deprivation of human and civil liberties, I can relate to the anger and frustration many of our people feel, however, when engage in conversation for solutions we uses handicapped excuses to continue to justify our negative actions or our epithetic in-actions and or when we confront those leaders within our community with power to take action, they rationalize or diminish it away; re-iterating the conditions, terms and values given by the dominant society.

2. The *availability bias* refers to people's tendency to think that examples of things that come readily to mind are more representative to the truth than is actually the case. The availability bias results from a cognitive shortcut known as the availability heuris-tic, defined as the reliance on those things that we immediately think of to enable quick decisions and judgments. That reliance helps us avoid laborious fact-checking and analysis but also increases the likelihood that our decisions will be flawed.

Naturally, the things that are most memorable can be brought to mind most quickly. However, there are a number of factors that influence how well we remember those things. For example, we tend to remember things that we observed ourselves more easily than things that we only heard about. For example, if the question was asked to a person concerning their relationship with their spouse or significant other, as far as 'how happy are they in their relationship' most likely their response would be drawn from their most recent interaction, rather negative or positive. Their response would be used as a summary of their relationship.

Not taking into account the "whole" relationship. If their most current experience was bad, that would cause them to most likely say that they are unhappy. Vice versa.

This is a natural human instinct; we are emotional people. However, when we reflect on our reality, we must reflect from its totality of living black in America. We must consider our suffering from the psychological displacement and cultural violence that arises from our interaction with white America. Our interpretation of events will be from our personal experiences and how society has shaped and effected our wounded identity (Post-Traumatic Stress).

3. The *hindsight bias* is a common cognitive bias that involved the tendency of people to see events, even random ones, as more predictable than they are. These are the people who tend to look back on events and believe that they "knew it all along", or "I told you so" ...we all got one of those friends.

4. The *self-serving bias* is when people tend to give themselves credit for successes but then lay the blame for failures on outside causes. When you do well on a project, you normally assume that it's because you worked hard. But when things don't turn out good, you are more likely to blame it on circumstances, other people or bad luck. This bias does serve an important role; it helps protect our self-esteem. However, it can often also lead to faulty attributions, such as blaming others for our own shortcomings.

Here are 5 simple steps that are great techniques that can be used to enhance your effective listening skill:

1. Provide the speaker with your undivided attention.

2. Be non-judgmental. Don't minimize or trivialize the speaker's issue.

3. Read the speaker. Observe the emotions behind the words. Is the speaker angry, afraid, frustrated or resentful? Respond to the emotion as well as the words.

4. Be Quiet. Don't feel you must have an immediate reply. Often if you allow for some quiet after the speaker has vented, they themselves will break the silence and offer a solution.

5. Assure your understanding. Ask clarifying questions and restate what you perceive the speaker to be saying.

Following these procedural steps will place you in a better situation for addressing the key issue and eliminated unwanted confrontation.

In order to get more out of listening during intense conversations, pay attention first: listen and give a brief restatement of what you have heard (especially feelings) before you express your own needs or position. The kind of listening recommended here separates acknowledging from approving or agreeing. Acknowledging another person's thoughts and feelings does not have to mean that you approve of or agree with that person's actions, positions, or way of expressing how they feel.

By listening and then repeating back in your own words the essence and feeling of what you have just heard, from their point of view, you allow them to feel the satisfaction of being understood, (a major human need). Listening responsively is always worthwhile as a way of letting people know that you care about them. The person who you are talking to will not automatically know how well you have understood them, and they may not be very good at asking for confirmation, unless you demonstrate and encourage them to open up honestly to you. You must keep in mind their experience and background which carries skepticism towards authoritative people. When a conversation is tense or difficult it is even more important to listen first and acknowledge what you hear. Otherwise, you will lose the chances of allowing transformation to take place in that person life and further, lose the opportunity for other to witness that connection.

"The art of listening starts with being quiet. "

- anonymous

When people are upset about something and want to talk about it, their capacity to listen is greatly diminished. Trying to get your point across to a person who is trying to express a strong feeling will usually cause the other person to try even harder to get their emotion recognized. Guess what? You will soon find yourself in a loud argument. On the other hand, once people feel that their messages and feelings have been heard, they start to relax, and they have more attention available for listening. So, under those types of situations you first must acknowledge their feelings.

The power of simple acknowledging. The practice of *responsive listening* described here separates acknowledging the thoughts and feelings that a person expresses from approving, agreeing, advising, or persuading. One recurring problem in conflict situations is that many people don't separate acknowledging from agreeing. They are joined together in people's minds. The effect of this is, let us say, that John feels that any acknowledgment of Fred's experience implies agreement and approval, therefore John will not acknowledge any of Fred's experience. Fred tries harder to be heard and John tries harder not to hear. Of course, this is a recipe for stalemate of going back and forth. We have all been in a situation like that.

People want both: to be *understood* and *acknowledged* on the one hand, and to be approved and agreed with, on the other. With practice, you can learn to respond first with a simple acknowledgment. As you do this, you may find that, figuratively speaking, you can give people half of what they want, even if you can't give them all of what they want. In many conflict situations that will be a giant step forward. You will also be more likely to acknowledge your position and experience, even if they don't sympathize with you. This mutual acknowledgment can create an emotional atmosphere in which it is easier to work toward agreement or more gracefully accommodate disagreements.

[6]

Re-Authoring Our Narratives
Redefining Your Story

During the 1980's social worker *Michael White* and *David Epston* developed a theory on narrative therapy. *White* and *Epston* believed that the six key elements of their theory if utilized effectively would give the people an opportunity to redefine who they are by helping them reconstruct their life narrative. *White* and *Epston* believed that narrative therapy is a form of psychotherapy that seeks to help people identify their strength, value and their own ability to control and confront any problems that they face. They believed that -

"The person is not the problem; rather the problem is the problem"

It would be our responsibility as facilitators, counselors, teachers or friend to help them co-author a new narrative about themselves by investigating the history of their stories through therapeutic conversation (group meetings or one-on-ones). People tend to internalized and accept the social narrative given to them defining their problem as part of the content of their character and as such they begin to believe that construct and look at themselves as deficits not seeing their potential that is not part of the conceptual narrative as strengths, skills and abilities that allowed them to survive, overcome, and deal with the problems that they were confronted with on a daily basis.

Looking at myself and how I self-internalized my story and rejected the narrative that was written about me and told about me. As I mention in my first book *"Breaking Though: Winning Against the Odds"* (chapter 5, pg 71)

"I can recall sitting in that cold court room listening during the sentencing phase of my trail how the judge and states attorney, who sentence me to prison, stated that I was unable to be rehabilitated, that I was unredeemable and unable to change. I was defined as a monster that was instrumental in creating terror within my community. I was only 17 years old when they said this, so basically, I was being written off and the sentence they gave me was meant to seal the deal. But the Most High had other plans. I look at my incarceration as Him setting me aside for bigger plans, and the real story of my life had not been written".

I am a prime example of the outcomes when we are taught how to externalized ourselves from the narrative and redefine the problem as separate from us and define the problem and let it sit where it should

– on society and see ourselves as "personal agents" who are charged with a responsibility to change the outcomes of our own situation.

Our narratives are reinforced through negative story telling; either through our own subjective experiences, or through the lenses of society media; news, televisions and movies. The African American current reality is a creation/created through these social constructs and through the shared stories of our experiences and as we tell and re-tell our stories, they help shape our self-identity and self-definition of who we are.

Externalization

The externalization process is more than simply a *"therapeutic technique for talking with people about their problems".* Externalizing conversations are the central foundation of our changing process involving the narrative approach.

Simply put, the Externalization process involves mainly teaching people how to separate themselves from the problem through conversation. When most people begin to evaluate themselves or their lives when things constantly seem to go wrong, they have already internalized the problem as if it's something wrong with them. The problem becomes a part of their identity. *(Carey & Russell,* 2002)

The first approach to separating the person from the problems start with allowing the person to explain the problem in their own language, you will only then modify the problem by objectifying it, then questioning the objectified problem – by looking at the problem in isolation and questioning the intention and goals relative to the person, then the person can begin to address the problem separate from any character issues that they may have associated to themselves as to why the problem existed. I was recently speaking with someone the other day, and he mentioned that he was having relationship problems and feels "stuck". The key externalized question I then begin to ask was, "are these issues of feeling "stuck" really about not being able to make a decision? Why are you feeling "stuck"? In this example, I begin to isolate "stuck" as the externalized key word. By simply engaging the client/student or group in an externalizing comfortable conversation and ask inspiring questions they will then see how you talk about the problem and how they been thinking about the problem. As you use externalizing language they will begin to think about their problems in an externalizing fashion. They will begin to distinctly separate themselves from their problems.

White & Epston (1990, p. 39) stated that "this practice 1. Decreases unproductive conflict between persons, including those disputes over who is responsible for the problem; 2. Undermines the sense of failure...; 3. Paves the way for cooperation...; 4. Open up new possibilities for people to take action to retrieve their lives and relationships from problems and its influences; 5. Frees people to take a lighter, more effective, and less stresses approached to problems; 6. Present options for dialoged, rather than monologue, about the problem.

The technique of externalizing is not an easy process due to the psychological damage many of us have suffered. It will take time to teach people how to re-organize their way of thinking about their situations. Be patient.

[7]

Wellness Wheel
The Holistic Approach to Self-Actualization

Wellness is both a dynamic process of physical, mental, and spiritual optimization and integration of the overall process of healing and transformation which will be incorporated with our model of changing the narrative. *Bill Hettler* (1984), who is considered the father of the modern-day wellness movement, defined wellness as *"an active process through which people become aware of and make choices towards a more successful existence" (Myers, Sweeney, and Witmer)* (2000).

As a person who works in an educational environment, I have witness teachers expecting children to jump right into their lessons upon arriving to school, which in most cases not reasonable because of the environment in which they live and just left. They then get frustrated as teachers, because the child seems uncooperative, not motivated and seems uninvolved. The children are then label and referred for an IEP evaluation. We must begin to relate to our children/student/clients from a perspective of trying to understand them from where they're at; mentally, socially, physically or spiritually. We must first understand their social factors and environments and try to incorporate the positive attributes of the wellness wheel in their lives.

We must recognize some of the current family dynamic that contribute to social dysfunctions we are witnessing in our youth that leaves them vulnerable to some of the risk factors and elements of society.

Understanding family structures:

Two family households are not the norm in our communities anymore. Family Fragmentation *(Scafidi,* 2008) exist

within 49% of most families according to U.S. Census data *(Pew Research Center* analysis of 2010).

This research states that adults 18- and older only represent 31% of marriages (Cohn, Passel, Wang and Livingston, 2011). Which is on a continual decline. Many adults according to this article choose to cohabitate or are single parent households. Due to this current trend, especially in the African American community, which represents 72% of single parent households; our children are missing out on the benefits of a two-parent household. Statistics reflects that children from two parent household (healthy relationships/marriages) benefit from being in a healthy stable environment and are more likely to have better physical and emotional health, show better school performance, have few behavioral problems in school, have better relationships with their mothers and fathers, lower likelihood of drug and alcohol abuse, shows lower rates of teen pregnancy, and shows a decrease in divorcing when they marry *(Adler-Baeder, Shirer & Bradford, 2007; Wilcox, Marquardt, Popenoe & Whitehead, 2011).*

In Breaking Through: Winning Against the Odds (Ross, K. 2015, pg. 78-89) I talk about the impact father's presence have in their children lives, even the negative impact due to their absence.

When I was growing up; which I grew up in a two-parent household, I learned from my parent who were married and were taught by their parents, that they were marrying for life, which values I learned. Yes, they had their ups and downs, yet, they stuck it out and did not air their problems out in public. This generation commitment to marriage is not as devoted because of the evolving values of society which has given them choices of easily opting out of their marriages. Society is not as committed to promoting and supporting marriage unless it's a 'new value' that challenges the traditional marriage values. Not to mention the "woman feminist movement" which has its own agenda that has cripple two parent households.

It's harder now for single parents to raise children being along with all the challenges now, then it was 20-30 years ago.

According to the *Annie E. Casey Foundation (2013)*, 67% of African American children are raised in single-parent families. A single-parent household faces more financial burdens then a two-parent household; single-parent children are more likely to suffer cognitive, emotional, and social problems; are more likely to fall below the poverty line; drop out of school and or become teen parents.

In *2009, Woman of Color Policy Network* reported the median income for single-parent female headed households was $26,457. They stated that "economic stress affects parenting as well as financial stability."

Poverty affects family functioning, such as disposition and optimism which contributes to dysfunctional families that transcends psychological trauma inherited intergenerationally. Intergenerational trauma can be passed through childhood experiences, hardships or economical stress/pressures (generational poverty), which these attributes can shape and effect interpersonal skills, parenting styles, and financial management skills, relationship skills, etc.

In two-parent households individuals have the benefit of having a partner to provide feedback, reinforcing positive attributes in child rearing and questioning negative ones. In isolation, a single parent will struggle, and questions their own ability to be good parents, especially if they did not grow up in a positive family environment with their parents as role models. As a result, single-parents are vulnerable to internalizing their problems, which will in most cases often affects their reaction to their children's behavioral issues.

So, with all this going on, I will be addressing some of these issues in the first phase of integrating the wellness wheel in the Breaking Through process, in my next book *The Ross Effect.*

The four phases of the wellness wheel wil include: a) introduction of the wellness model; b) assessment of individual wellness; c) designing and implementing interventions; and d) evaluation and follow up.

The wellness wheel four outcomes:

1.   Building Successful Learners

2.   Building Strong Confident Individuals

3.   Building Effective Contributors to the Community

4.   Building Responsible Citizens

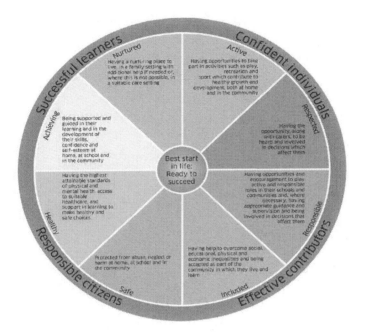

You should integrate the eight internal cycles of the wellness wheel to bring about building and changing the cultural mentality that will help you achieve your own self-actualization:

1. *Nurtured* - understand your environment and ensure that your environment offers you the essential

elements that would allow you to learn and grow and feel secured.

2. *Active* - become active in extra curriculum activity that promotes health and community involvement.

3. *Respect* – be assertive and be voiceful in all decision that affects you.

4. *Responsible* – take an active and responsible role in your school and community and give guidance and supervision to others when necessary to help them make better decision that affect them and encourage them to take responsibility for their own actions.

5. *Included* - overcome social, educational, and economical inequalities become inclusive in the community when necessary.

6. *Safety* - Talk about "being safe and feeling safe" at home, in the community and at school. Share advice and strategies to your children or children in the community on avoiding danger and to control their own safety.

7. *Health* - Discuss the principles of attaining high standards of physical and mental health that comes from making healthy and safe choices with your family.

8. *Achieving* - Give support, guidance and acknowledgement to our younger generation in their learning and development of their skills; help them build their confidence and self-esteem at home, school and the community.

The correlation of having a healthy outlook on life despite your environmental circumstance is essential to overcoming the problem. Most prognosticators have written you off and have summed your life up as "worthless", "a lost cause", "there's nothing that can be done", "it's too late", etc. I was written off at the young age of sixteen and sentence to serve forty years in prison. It was said by those who held my fate in their hands "that I was un-redeemable", "beyond able to be rehabilitated". So, their sentence was designed to seal my fate. How many young men in our community feel this way? Society sends this message to our youth in all type of subliminal ways. Therefore it is our duty to erase this message and teach them to re-record a new message of "I can make it", "I will be successful in spite of my challenges", "I will survive", "I will not succumb to a spiritual death of complacency", "I will not be a product of my environment, if anything, my environment will motivate me to succeed".

The *Breaking Through: Changing the Narrative* is built upon the foundation of cognitive behavior therapy and cognitive behavior modification. We MUST change the behavior to change the outcomes.

What is Cognitive Behavioral Therapy? Cognitive behavioral therapy basic tenants are:

➢ The way people structure and interpret their experiences, will determines their mood and behaviors.

➢ Changing people's conceptualization lies at the heart of cognitive behavioral therapy.

➤ Cognitive therapy rest upon the belief that "how a person thinks will determine how that person will feel, and how that person feels will dictate how that person will behave".

[8]

Challenging the Spirit Within
To develop a positive attitude

Our attitude has a profound effect on the quality of our life. Optimism and pessimism create two completely different realities. The one that exist in many African American communities around the country imposed by racism and discrimination, and the one that extends beyond those boundaries that many have been able to escape. By taking a few simple steps to adopt a more optimistic and positive attitude, you can enjoy the immediate and long-term benefits of making your dreams and goals a reality.

Charles Duhigg explains in his book *"The Power of Habit: Why We Do What We Do and How to Change It"*, states that *"it is easier for someone to establish good habits, and change poor ones, when they are part of a group (community). One reason why groups are so powerful in helping people to change behavior is that they help people see that change is possible (e.g. they see that it happens in others like them), which then makes it easier to believe that change is possible. Belief in the ability to change is critical to change. If you have seen change in other people as a result of participating in a positive group that promote growth and development, you should know firsthand about the power of groups".*

"Every successful individual knows that his or her achievement depends on a community of people working together"

Paul Ryan

Chicago Chapter of The Big Homies Club mentoring session (2018)

Critical Discussion on Black Male Masculinity vs. Manhood (right to left: Hip Hop Detox founder Enoch Mohammed, William "Billy" Moore, case manger at Green Re-entry, Sis. Daphne Jackson, Community Activist and Anthony Lowery, the Safer Foundation (6/2018)

Trinity UCC Child Care Centers, Inc (Chicago) Fatherhood Engagement Group meeting (2018)

In my book *"The Ross Effect"*, I dedicate a module on how to internalize your positive energy and turn your negatives into positives. Your situation is based upon your perception of it. Your perception of your situation whether good or bad will cause you to respond in a certain way; as I mentioned earlier in a previous chapter that we are all influenced by our environment. Our environment creates our realities - meaning that it shapes our view of the world. I think as parents we can do an injustice to our children when we attempt to educate them on racism and discrimination. Do not misunderstand me; I am only speaking on how we teach these lessons. Unconsciously we can transfer our fears and anger to our children, and they grow up looking at the world through our eyes. Not from a perspective of strength and strategies but from a position of anger, hopelessness and despair, if we teach those lessons wrongly.

Tupac Shakur created a term in the 1990's describing how America's racism and discriminatory policies created psychological damage within the African American community that effects our interaction and relationship with society. It's a relationship of mistrust and deceit. Which materialize in many young people rebellious mentality. *Tupac* coined the phrase *"THUG LIFE"* the acronym describing how systemic injustices over generations indoctrinates our youth to grow up with anger. *T.H.U.G. L.I.F.E. "the hate you gave little infants fucks everybody"*, which he was referring to how society through her actions educated us (feed us) her hatred and as a result we grow-up with that same malicious, violent hatred. Earlier I spoke on everything revolves around a cause and effect world. What you put out will eventually return. Its karma. However, even though our environment is reflective of the society we grow up in, we control our own thoughts and how we internalize information. The 2018 movie created from author *Angie Thomas* 2017 best selling book entitle *"The Hate You Gave"* show a father who was an ex-gang member, experiencing his struggle raising his children in a cultural of discrimination, police brutality, and gangs. In his effort to educate his children he did not educate them from a position of weakness, but from a position of power by ensuring that they knew and understood the Black Panther ten-point platform. By doing so, he was instilling in them a value system of advocacy and strength. Despite this father background, he understood his role and responsibility as a father and as a member of the community at large.

Let's be truthful and internalize our own faults and shortcomings. When we begin to do that then we can put ourselves and others in a position of power and transformation. We cannot continue to blame others for our own failures. No one is responsible for your success, but you! Let me repeat this...No one is responsible for your success, but you! For far too long we have paid a heavy price for not understanding this.

So, as of today you must commit to yourself as you move forward that you will be responsible for your own actions. This must be a personal commitment, because without this affirmation you will continue to go through life blaming others for your own faults. There are certain things that I see in our community that I do not agree with, and that is the lack of accountability among each other. We must begin to hold each other to a higher standard based upon edicts and principles that promote love for each other through the promotion of social development; financial stewardship through economic development and support for black own businesses; community safety of our children, and our elders; education and awareness through community-based organizations committed to creating a forum for the community. Now, what I am mentioning is not a new concept, these things are being done, they are only being mention now is because YOU must commit to becoming a part of this movement and transformation to impact your life. You are part of the whole, and in order for you as an individual to grow, you must reconnect to the whole (the body) and we must all be on one accord moving as one.

What motivates you? We are motivated by our value system, our value system is motivated by our emotions, our emotions motivate our actions. Our emotions are defined through our story telling. Remember earlier when I was talking about narrative therapy? Our story enables us to communicate how we feel about certain matters. Our stories are not abstract, they are about real-life experiences that has the power to move us in a certain direction. We must be careful of our storytelling, because if we continue to tell our story the wrong way it can cause inertia, apathy, fear, isolation and self-doubt. You must redefine your story and tell it from a strength base approach on how you were challenged, but, overcame and survive. Your story communicates who you are, the choices that shaped your character, and the values you hold that influenced those choices. Learning to tell your story demands the courage of introspect, and even more the courage of sharing what you discovered.

As a people we have this internal trait that is called *Emotional Resiliency* that gives us strength to make it through our tough times...we as a people have experienced all types of attacks, challenges and setbacks, yet, we survived and overcame them- and we are here. So, when you tell your story tell it from a strength base perspective.

[9]

My Future-My Terms
Proper-Preparation-Prevents-Poor-Performances

Have you given any thought about your life? How you want to live? Where will you live? Will you buy a house or live in an apartment? What type of job you want? How much money you want to make? Will you go to college? What type of degree you will need to be who you want to be, or do you need a degree? What will you do once you are released from prison, grow up, get married, etc.?

Some of these questions may seem overwhelming depending on your age; however, it's never too early or too late to give though to these questions. It's

best to consider these questions now then rather

waiting till later. You must begin to discover your

options and develop a plan as soon as possible.

Proper-Preparation-Prevents-Poor-Performances. I

mention In Breaking Through: Winning Against the

Odds, how many of us live our lives wrong. We go

through life without a plan. We freestyle through

life. What's your plan? Take the time now to go

through this Breaking Through exercise. Write

down your response on a separate sheet of paper.

The Breaking Through Exercise #1

1. Do I have a purpose in life and what is my pur-

pose?

2. What motivates me and keeps me going every day?

3. What's holding me back from achieving my goals and reaching my potential?

4. Who are some of the people that influence you to be successful?

5. What will be your measure of success?

6. Are you satisfied with your life right now? Why or why not? What are you planning to do about it?

7. If you can choose to be anybody in the world, who would you choose to be and why?

8. What would you like to achieve in life?

9. How would you want to be remembered?

10. What is your short-term goal for this year? Come up with a SMART goal using the worksheet (not included). (Specific, Measurable, Attainable, Relevant, and Time-Bound)

"It's never too late to turn it all around. Be Honest with yourself and others. If anything, you're doing in life is not what you should be doing.... Stop.

Life is way too short to continue in the wrong direction, but the longer that you do the less time you'll have to travel in the right direction."

- Man of Honor

Most people have thought about their future when they were young, they had big dreams which they wanted to realize some day. Some have now, as adults reached their dreams, and some have fallen short. We have all had dreams about interesting job that paid hug salaries, we had dreams about having a loving family, having a beautiful house and many friends. Our future back then as a child was often an escape from our usual ordinary live, we lived and played in make believe worlds. For some of us those dreams became a part of our goals to escape our circumstances and conditions that we grew up in.

All of us share a desire to live the most productive and fulfilling lives possible. However, in order to do that, we must believe that our success is determined by our own inner desire for self-determination; which means that we must play an active role in shaping our own lives. Self-determination is defined as "a people who have the ability to control his or her own destiny," which is a significant change from an approach in which we expect those who do not have our interest at heart to make decisions for us to secure our future. Self-determination must encourage us to develop the necessary attitudes,

skills and knowledge that will empower us to control, as much as possible, our own destiny.

The following characteristic are trademarks of self-determination, and are qualities that you need to develop in order to be successful:

Attitudes and Beliefs

- Self-confidence

- Self-esteem

- Feeling valued by others

- Internal Locus of Control

- Self-determination

- Positive Outlooks

Skills

- Goal setting skills

- Decision-making skills

- Self-Advocacy

- Problem-solving skills

- Self-regulation

- Social skills

- Communication skills

- Independent living

Knowledge

- Knowledge of self

- Knowledge of resources and the system

- Knowledge of rights and responsibilities

- Perceived Options

I would like for you to follow this *Breaking Through Exercise* for you to internalize the thoughts of situations where you were either not in control of your destiny or felt as if your future was being determined by others. Use a separate sheet of paper to write your answers.

Breaking Through Exercise #2

HOW CAN SELF-DETERMINATION HELP ME?

Name an experience you had when you were not in control; when someone else had control over something that was important to you.

How did it feel NOT to be in control?

Identify feelings you might have had when you were not in control:

Powerless - Frustrated – Incompetent - Depressed – Angry - Belligerent - Helpless

Name an experience you had when you were in control over something that was important to you.

Name some feelings you might have had when you were in control:

Powerful - Motivated - Excited - A little scared - Responsible – Alive

Think of self-determination as being in charge of your own life.

Breaking Through Exercise #3

Task 1: Match the halves of these proverbs about the future:

Tomorrow is   at forty

Eat, drink, and, be, merry,   what you can do today

Life begins   for tomorrow never comes

Live for today,   to old to learn

Never put off until tomorrow   another day

The child is   the father of the man

You are never   for tomorrow we die

Task 2: Put these events of human's life in the correct order:

1) Get married   6) get separated

2) Graduate from university   7) die

3) Be born   8) get divorced

4) Have children   9) go to school

5) Find a job   10) retire

Task 3: What are these people's plans for the future? Match the direct speech to the people.

1) "When I grow up, I will be an astronaut and I'll fly to Mars and live there."

2) "I have just retired, so I am going to spend more time doing the things I like and spending more time with my grandchildren."

3) "We got engaged yesterday and we're getting married this summer."

4) "The holidays are starting, so I am going to relax and get ready spend time with the family."

5) "We are playing an important football match to-morrow, so I am going to bed early this evening."

a) Barbara (60 yrs. old)

b) Frank (25 yrs. old)

c) Henry (6 yrs. old)

d) Mary (17 yrs. old)

e) Paul and Miriam (41 and 35 yrs. old)

1	2	3	4	5
C (example)				

(a,b,c,d, or e)

These may seem like some real simple exercises, right? But observe yourself or others on the order of how they planned or set goals concerning their life or successes they achieve. You will quickly find out that they had a order to things and how their goals was accomplished

[10]

Who Am I
What is my Purpose

When considering your goals, consider your strengths and the things you do best. Character strengths are very important when you consider and look at the lives of those who are successful. Your strengths are tangible, and concrete. They are not lucid as when you consider the things that make you happy. Your happiness should not be based upon the feeling of pleasure in the "moment", like the pleasure that comes from "liquor, drugs, woman, music, and material things" those pleasure is short lived and fades away and will cause you to continue to search for that "high" or first feeling again. I once termed this as "escaping reality" and "living in suspended animation". Sometime our dissatisfaction leads us to finding alternative therapy of coping with life.

Bridget Greenville-Cleave in her book "A Practical Guide: Positive Psychology", talks about the distinction of "being happy" or "feeling happy".

"But beware of this about callings: they may not lead us where we intended to go or even where we want to go. If we choose to follow, we may have to be willing to let go of the life we already planned and accept whatever is waiting for us. And if the calling is true, though we may not have gone where we intended, we will surely end up where we need to be."
— *Steve Goodier*

Finding or accepting your purpose in life is a difficult task. For many we escape the calling by ignoring it, because as most "callings" they require us to make great sacrifices of ourselves. Then the other part is that we surround ourselves with people who do not aspire to be anything other than who they are.

I was listening to Prince Ea, a motivational speaker the other day, and he was telling a story about this eagle being raised by chickens. He starts off with a man finding a eagles egg and placing the eagle egg among chickens so it will hatch with the chicken eggs, and once the eagle hatched it was raised a chicken, doing all the things that chicken does, it ate like a chicken, plucked like a chicken and even walked like a chicken. Until one day the eagle seen a majestic bird flying so gracefully up in the sky, the eagle asked the other chickens "what was that", the other chickens responded by saying "oh that's an eagle, don't worry you can never fly like that". The eagle never learned that he was an eagle and he eventually died a chicken, never learning that he was that majestic bird.

This story was so powerful and is so true for a lot of people who die not knowing who they are and their true potential; they rely on what others tell them who they are.

The reality of this eagle life may have not been pleasant at all, but because others around him didn't see his unique difference, or his potential and desire to be different, they convinced him that he was just like them, so, he settle for just being a chicken.

Sometimes we must listen to our dissatisfactions; our dissatisfactions are a result of our introspection. If we are dissatisfied after we have evaluated our lives, or the situations we are in, then good, because only when we are honest with ourselves, we find the power to change our lives.

I do a lot of reflection in my own life, and sometimes I must admit my own dissatisfaction at times on how things turn out when I am involved in certain situations.

Over the past few years I haven't been "all-good" all the time. I have experience depression and unhappy feelings many times when I think about it. But then, I have to catch myself, and start looking at things from a whole different perspective. I pride myself for having a deeply spiritual connection that causes me to have a great gratitude for being blessed in so many ways, coming from where I been. So, in times of chaos, depression, grief or loss, I can find solace in knowing that all things will work itself out. I made a promise a long time ago to someone I deeply loved; my mother, Dorothy Ross, that I would never ever fall short of my potential again, and in order to keep that promise I had to let go of my own since of control and listen to that higher wisdom that was beyond me and within me – God, and trust the process...

I can truly say that I have a profound sense of gratitude for how my life is unfolding. I sit on my front porch during the evenings, listening to the wind as it blows, or the cars as they drive pass, or the other noise from the creatures of the night as they settle down, an as I sip on a drink and smoking on my stogie (cigar) looking up at the stars in the sky, I smile and count myself among the blessed.

Most of our dissatisfaction is as a result of us not meeting our own potentials in life. We are either angry or have anxiety. Research has shown that our sense of dissatisfaction triggers our flight/fight mechanism, bringing anxiety, displaced activity, and the danger of making life-changing decisions from a fear-based place. And no matter how we try to mask it, or replace it with any alternative escapism, the feeling will not go away until we begin to see it for the *evolutionary energy* that it is.

Seeing it from this perspective of being a form of *evolutionary energy* will cause us to make the necessary changes in our lives or accept the things need accepting. If we recognize the energy of dissatisfaction as an evolutionary imperative, then we can begin not to take it personally, because its not personal, per se. it's the universe speaking to our souls. Listen!

In closing I want to share a poem by a young sister

from Chicago entitle "Who am I?"

<u>Who am I?</u>

Who am I?
Am I my appearance?
Did you see only my body when I spoke?
Is that why you didn't hear it?
Perhaps my identity lies in my backside
Because according to your prejudgment
That's where my personality hides
Who am I?
Am I my tanned skin?
The colored shell that I dwell in?
Maybe I am my community
You know, every struggled black family
I know this is a hard question to answer
But the more you look, you never analyze her
No, me
You never analyze me
You only assume who I am based on the physical
things you see
I s that why I'm "ghetto?"
Because my skin is black?
You sit back and say "no"
But actually discovering who I am is something you
lack
Who am I?
Am I the violence of my city?
You know, all of Chicago's shootings and the police

brutality?
Like, I would really like to know
What's my identity, though?
Is it how tall or short I am?
Or how you see me as a hater or a fan?
Who am I?
Because there isn't much to it
You saw my brown skin and said that you knew it
You "knew" who I was
You "knew" I was street because I didn't say "cousin",
I said "cuz"
And no matter how many time I say
The person I am doesn't lie in the physical
You push my words away
And say that my words aren't meaningful
So I sit here confused
Because I don't know who I am
So I don't know what to do
So again I ask
Who am I?
Because everyday I'm told I am my facial expression
Despite the fact that my smile
Hides my depression
And for you it doesn't take a while
No not at all
When you see people you know who they are
So again, to you I call
Who am I?
I asked if it was my appearance
And you acted like you didn't hear it
I asked if it was my race
And you you said it wasn't my place
I asked if it was my city

And you just wondered if anyone ever asked me
I go on and on
Trying to find out who I am
And every Suggestion I made was wrong
So right now I decide to take my stand
Who am I?
Was the question I asked
And you answered based
On irrelevant things
So every word I say
Will come out the same way
To let you know
That I am not my black shell
Or how loud I yell
It's the personality
Not my body
So when I ask
"Who am I?"
You shouldn't think
You know me based off of the color of my skin
You should get
To know me based on the person I am from within
For the very last time,
This question is what I will repeat
And when you answer don't only look
Me up and down
From my head to my feet
Look in my eyes
Deep enough to see the personality inside
So,
Who am I?

— Mackenzie Askew

Bibliography

Adler-Baeder, Shirer & Bradford, (2007) *What love got to do with it: The role of healthy couple relationships and marriages in promoting child, family, and community well-being. The Forum for Family and Consumer Issues, 12 (1).*

Akbar, N., *(2006) Breaking the Chain of Psychological Slavery 6th ed.*

Annie E. Casey Foundation, (2103) *More Children Living In Single Parent Households*

Carry, M., and Russell, M., (2002) *Externalizing: Commonly asked questions*

Cohn, Passel, Wing and Livingston (20011). *PEW Research: Soccial and Demographic Trends*

Covey R. S., *(1989) The Seven Habit of Highly Effective People*

Davey, M., (2016) *The New York Times: Memorial Day Weekend Violence in Chicago*

DeGruy, J., (2005). Posttraumatic Slave Syndrome*: America's Legacy of Enduring Injury and Healing*

Diagnostic of Statistical Book of Mental Disorders *(DSM-V) (2015)*

Duhigg, C., (2012) *The Power of Habit: Why We Do What We Do In Life And Business*

Fanon, F. (1952) *Black Skin White mask*

Fussiun, P., Rejas, M., Serkis, L., Pele, I & Hirsch, S. (2003*) Family approach with grandchildren of holocaust survivors, America Journal of Psychology, 57(4), 519-527)*

Granville, B. (2012) *Practical Guide: Positive Psychology*

Harman, J. (1997) *Trauma and Recovery: The Aftermath of Violence-From Domestic Abuse to Potential Terror*

Hettler, B. (1984) *Six Dimension of The Wellness Wheel*

Maslow, A. (1943*) Hierarchy of Needs*

Myers, J.E., Sweeney, T.J., and Witmer, M. *(2000) The Wheel of Wellness Counseling for Wellness: A Holistic Model for Treatment Planning*

Pew Research Center (2010) *Household and Family Structure*

Ross, K., (2015) *Breaking Through: Winning Against the Odds*

Scafidi, B. (2008) *Fragmentation of Two-Family Households*

Skinner, B.F. (1984) *Selection By Consequence*

The Chicago Tribune (2016) *Chicago Memorial Day weekend Violence*

Thomas, A. (2017) *The Hate You Give*

White, M., and Epston, D. (1990) *Narrative Therapy*

Wilcox, D.B., Marquardet, E., Popenoe, D., and Whitehead, K.D. (2011) *Money & Marriage: National Marriage Project*

Woman of Color Policy Network (2009) *Affirmative Action in the Age of Obama*

ABOUT THE AUTHOR

Breaking Through was inspired by my experiences and challenges trying to reintegrate into society after serving 23 1/2 years in prison. Over the years the journey has been difficult, yet, I was able to overcome those challenges and have now conquered my fears and have achieved many of my goals.

I hold a master's degree in counseling and attend speaking engagements sharing my story. It is my belief that many who share in my experience can learn from the methods I used to overcome my challenges.

Breaking Through: Changing the Narrative is my second book on motivation and challenging young men to channel that negative character attributed to their environment to positive energy to change their narrative. It is my hope in this book that I deliver what I aspire to give.

My experiences are no different than the average black male who has experienced incarceration. The only difference is how I did not allow my past to define who I could become. I broke through those barriers.

I now use my blessings and the opportunity to share my story, and to give guidance to those who are going through challenging times and who are finding it difficult to navigate their way from the streets, gang and drug culture that hold many of them captive.

I don't define myself as a therapist; I am only sharing a story and a method of how my plan worked for me.

Made in the USA
Middletown, DE
23 February 2022

61716994R00099